IS PLASTIC MY FOOD

First Edition 2018

Copyright Madhvi4EcoEthics

PREFACE

My book, "Is Plastic My Food?" tells about the Plastic Pollution happening in the world. I want to inspire kids to protect the environment in our planet Earth.

I wrote and illustrated this book when I was 5 years and 9 months old. The Appendix has some images of the real-world Plastic Pollution and its effects on Albatross colonies and other species in the ecosystem.

Madhvi Chittoor
Arvada, CO, USA
Feb 21, 2018

I am Alta, the Albatross. I live in an island called Midway, in the Pacific Ocean. I swoop into the waters of the ocean with my huge wings to catch fish.

But along with fish, plastic pieces are going into my beak. Then they end up in my tummy and I can't digest them. I get tummy aches. The same thing happens to my whole colony of friends.

I will soon die, and so will my friends and all albatrosses would gradually become extinct.

Please save me and my friends. Plastic is not my food. Recycle existing plastic and refuse new plastic. Invent and use biodegradable products.

No Plastics Allowed!!

APPENDIX

The pictures below are some real-world pictures of the Plastic Pollution in the Oceans.

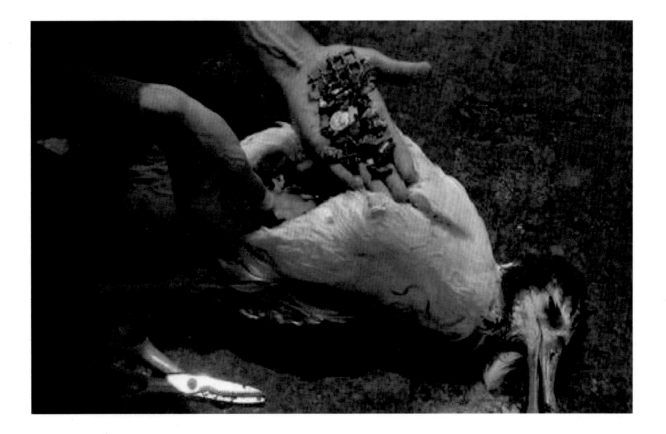

13

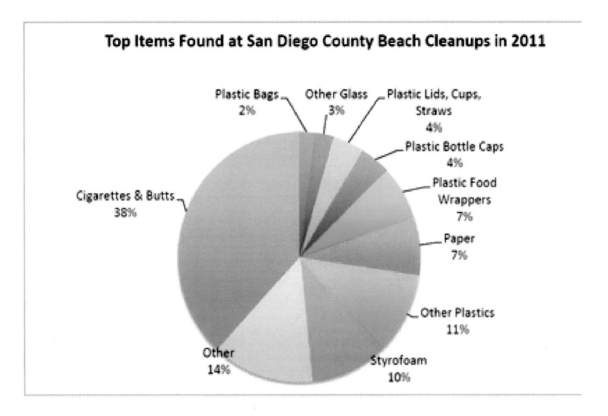

Top Items Found at San Diego County Beach Cleanups in 2011

- Plastic Bags 2%
- Other Glass 3%
- Plastic Lids, Cups, Straws 4%
- Plastic Bottle Caps 4%
- Plastic Food Wrappers 7%
- Paper 7%
- Other Plastics 11%
- Styrofoam 10%
- Other 14%
- Cigarettes & Butts 38%

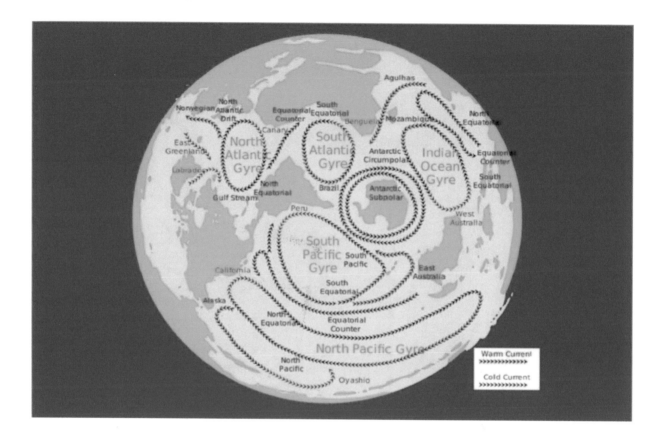

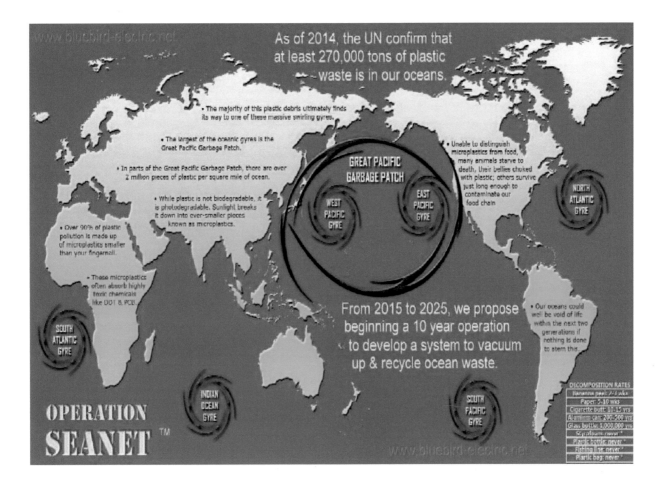

The Truth About
Styrofoam

It might keep your coffee hot without burning your hand, but plastic foam – more commonly known as Styrofoam – is one of the most harmful materials around when it comes to the environment. This petroleum-based plastic has gained a lot of negative attention in recent years, prompting bans in many cities such as New York City and Washington D.C.

52113109R00018

Made in the USA
Columbia, SC
26 February 2019